MARK & TRACE ANALYSIS

SOLVING CRIMES WITH SCIENCE:
Forensics

Computer Investigation
Criminal Psychology & Personality Profiling
DNA Analysis
Document Analysis
Entomology & Palynology
Explosives & Arson Investigation
Fingerprints, Bite Marks, Ear Prints
Forensic Anthropology
Forensics in American Culture
Mark & Trace Analysis
Pathology
Solving Crimes With Physics

MARK & TRACE ANALYSIS

William Hunter

Mason Crest

Mason Crest
450 Parkway Drive, Suite D
Broomall, PA 19008
www.masoncrest.com

Printed and bound in the United States of America.

First printing
9 8 7 6 5 4 3 2 1

Series ISBN: 978-1-4222-2861-6
ISBN: 978-1-4222-2871-5
ebook ISBN: 978-1-4222-8957-0

The Library of Congress has cataloged the
hardcopy format(s) as follows:

Library of Congress Cataloging-in-Publication Data

Hunter, William, 1971-
  Mark & trace analysis / William Hunter.
      p. cm. — (Solving crimes with science, forensics)
  Audience: 012.
  Audience: Grades 7 to 8.
  Includes bibliographical references and index.
  ISBN 978-1-4222-2871-5 (hardcover) — ISBN 978-1-4222-2861-6 (series) — ISBN 978-1-4222-8957-0 (ebook)
  1. Forensic sciences—Juvenile literature. 2. Trace analysis—Juvenile literature. 3. Trace evidence—Juvenile literature. 4. Evidence, Criminal—Juvenile literature. 5. Criminal investigation—Juvenile literature. I. Title. II. Title: Mark and trace analysis.
  HV8073.8.H789 2014
  363.25'62—dc23
                              2013006962

Produced by Vestal Creative Services.
www.vestalcreative.com

Contents

Introduction

By Jay A. Siegel, Ph.D.
Director, Forensic and Investigative Sciences Program
Indiana University, Purdue University, Indianapolis

It seems like every day the news brings forth another story about crime in the United States. Although the crime rate has been slowly decreasing over the past few years (due perhaps in part to the aging of the population), crime continues to be a very serious problem. Increasingly, the stories we read that involve crimes also mention the role that forensic science plays in solving serious crimes. Sensational crimes provide real examples of the power of forensic science. In recent years there has been an explosion of books, movies, and TV shows devoted to forensic science and crime investigation. The wondrously successful *CSI* TV shows have spawned a major increase in awareness of and interest in forensic science as a tool for solving crimes. *CSI* even has its own syndrome: the "*CSI* Effect," wherein jurors in real cases expect to hear testimony about science such as fingerprints, DNA, and blood spatter because they saw it on TV.

The unprecedented rise in the public's interest in forensic science has fueled demands by students and parents for more educational programs that teach the applications of science to crime. This started in colleges and universities but has filtered down to high schools and middle schools. Even elementary school students now learn how science is used in the criminal justice system. Most educators agree that this developing interest in forensic science is a good thing. It has provided an excellent opportunity to teach students science—and they have fun learning it! Forensic science is an ideal vehicle for teaching science for several reasons. It is truly multidisciplinary; practically every field of science has forensic applications. Successful forensic scientists must be good problem solvers and critical thinkers. These are critical skills that all students need to develop.

In all of this rush to implement forensic science courses in secondary schools throughout North America, the development of grade-appropriate resources that help guide students and teachers is seriously lacking. This new series: *Solving Crimes With Science: Forensics* is important and timely. Each book in the series contains a concise, age-appropriate discussion of one or more areas of forensic science.

Students are never too young to begin to learn the principles and applications of science. Forensic science provides an interesting and informative way to introduce scientific concepts in a way that grabs and holds the students' attention. *Solving Crimes With Science: Forensics* promises to be an important resource in teaching forensic science to students twelve to eighteen years old.

INTRODUCING . . . FORENSIC SCIENCE!

In 1936, the wife of an NBC executive was killed in her New York City apartment, strangled with her own pajama top. The killer left her body, bound with twine, in the bathroom. Investigators believed she had known the killer because of the lack of evidence of a struggle. A single white hair was found on the floor of the bedroom.

Microscopic examination indicated it was a horse hair. A local company had delivered a horsehair couch earlier that day, and the deliverymen had reported the crime to the police. The police, investigating all leads, collected a sample of twine used by the furniture company. It turned out to be a match to the type of twine used to tie up the victim. The police were able to determine that the distributor of the twine only sold their product to one company in the city: the same one that had delivered the couch.

Armed with this evidence, investigators began looking at the day's activities for the two men who had delivered the couch. One of the two men was unable to give a solid alibi, and police began to pressure him with the evidence. He eventually confessed to the killing and was quickly convicted. The man was sent to jail for the remainder of his life—all because of clues collected by forensic science.

You might be surprised by just how much information a skilled and knowledgeable investigator can gather from a seemingly empty room! Even the most thorough criminal makes mistakes because it is nearly impossible to control all of the possible sources of physical evidence. Sometimes, a single

Traces of rope or twine found on a victim's remains can lead investigators to a suspect.

Ancient Egyptians tried to deter grave robbers by placing warnings on tombs.

tiny bit of evidence can be enough to solve a crime. Every piece of evidence, no matter how small, found at a crime scene is commonly grouped together as "trace evidence." Criminalists are the experts tasked with gathering and examining these super-small sources of information. They, like other forensic scientists, use their knowledge to solve crimes. In today's world, forensics is a fast-growing field—but crime-solving is as ancient as civilization.

Introducing . . . Forensic Science!   11

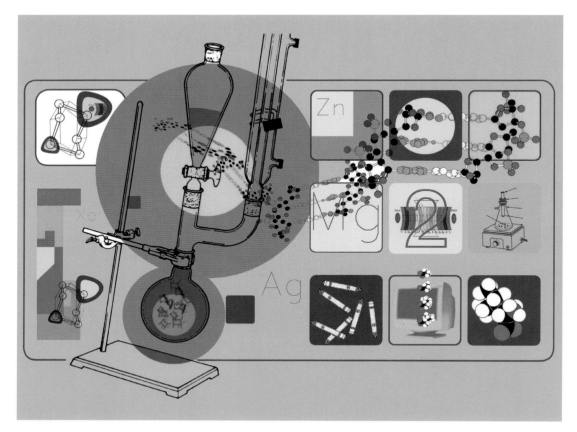

A forensic scientist examines clues without bias.

Written history's long record has numerous references to crime of one sort or another. People have always wanted to deter criminals, and failing that, to catch them. For example, ancient Egyptian tombs contain multiple warnings about the wrath of the gods if the contents of the tombs are disturbed; the mummy's curse is still mentioned at archaeological digs at the pyramids. Individuals caught stealing were severely punished and often killed for their deeds—but the biggest problem then—as now—was proving the guilt of the accused.

In the old days, criminal trials were sometimes less than fair. People were often punished for crimes based on the word of one or two individuals, with little concern given to sorting out the truth of the affair. Evidence was almost unheard of. Advances in science have opened the door for much more effective evidence discovery, however. We now call the work of those who seek to solve crimes using scientific technology and knowledge forensic science.

Few areas in the realm of science are as widespread and important as forensic science. When a crime is committed, it often falls to the forensic scientist to examine the clues—the evidence—and to try to determine the identity of the criminal. A highly trained and specialized professional, the best forensic scientist is capable of using the tiniest amount of evidence to give insights into a case. *Forensic science* is a unique area of science. No one can dispute the importance of the contributions to society made by forensic science; the ability to solve crime is undeniably important.

Almost everyone has heard of forensic science, but few truly understand the way it operates. Television shows like *CSI* have brought forensic science into the public eye over the last few years, glamorizing this not-always glamorous work. The experts on these shows are often crime-solving super-heroes, going from crime scene to crime scene and toting guns while working the case. "Real-world" forensic science is rarely a tooth-and-nail drama. While it is true that crime-scene specialists exist and the work they do is very important, scientists are seldom sent to investigate the crime scene, and even more rarely do they interrogate witnesses. Most of the specialists work under carefully controlled conditions in well-stocked laboratories at a central forensic lab.

Forensic science is not, however, a boring science. Few other scientific disciplines can claim links to as much of the real world as can forensic science. Forensic scientists work in one of the most demanding and rewarding fields of science in the world. After all, at the end of each workday, not many people can lay claim to having truly helped make society safer!

Introducing . . . Forensic Science! 13

The Use of Forensic Science

Forensic science can be used to help solve legal cases, be they *civil* or *criminal* in nature. The majority of forensic cases are criminal, but there has been a recent increase in the use of forensic techniques in civil cases, as the costs of examining evidence have decreased. Evidence must be treated with the utmost care, because forensic results can change a person's life forever.

Forensic science covers a broad spectrum of subjects, from finding the tiniest bits of evidence at a crime scene to testifying about evidence in court. A trained investigator often finds a number of different types of evidence, including biological samples such as saliva or blood, chemical samples like gasoline, and physical evidence like pieces of glass or paint chips.

The forensic scientist's job is to analyze the evidence collected from crime scenes, looking for clues that might help solve crimes. She examines evidence that can change the course of a trial, either for the prosecution or the defense, so it is very important for a forensic scientist to be impartial and objective at all times. A professional evidence examiner must not allow her personal feelings to affect the results of her examination. More than

The United States Federal Bureau of Investigation (FBI) maintains a handbook of forensic methods and techniques for use by all states in the country. Most state crime laboratories refer to this work as the definitive standard for the analysis of evidence. In the handbook, there are hundreds of different techniques and guidelines for their usage.

Broken glass is a type of evidence that can be used in an investigation.

one criminal case has been thrown out of court after it was discovered that the forensic examiner had strong personal feelings about the guilt of the accused and allowed the results of his efforts to be biased by these feelings.

Introducing . . . Forensic Science!   **15**

In 1686, Marcello Malpighi, a professor of anatomy at the University of Bologna in Italy and founder of comparative physiology, first noted the characteristics of fingerprints. He detailed the patterns of ridges and made hypotheses about the development of the specific characteristics of his own fingerprints, but he did not connect fingerprints to the ability to identify individuals. It would be many years before anyone thought to use fingerprints in criminal cases.

The History of Forensic Science

The earliest recorded use of forensic science dates back to ancient China, where people used fingerprints as proof of identity in barters. Many sculptors placed a fingerprint impression in their clay sculptures to prove it was their work. The first text referring to the use of forensic science techniques, *Hsi Duan Yu* (literally translated as "the washing away of wrongs") was published in about 700 CE. It contained writings about methods of determining whether a person had been strangled or drowned. Killers sometimes strangled a victim and then plunged the body into a pond or other body of water to cover their tracks, relying on the fact that people found in water were assumed to have died accidentally. The work of early forensic scientists in the *Hsi Duan Yu* became the basis for solving these types of crimes.

Physical matching of two or more pieces of evidence was first documented in 1784, when an English inspector assigned to investigate a mur-

The study of fingerprints to prove identity dates back to ancient China.

der was able to match a small scrap of newsprint found in a suspect's pocket to a shred of newsprint caught on a sharp edge of the murder weapon, a pistol found near the crime scene. Using careful observation, the inspector created a detailed comparison of the similarities and identifying marks shared by the two pieces of paper. The result was a murder conviction in an otherwise puzzling case.

The discovery that physical matching could be forensically useful led to a cascade of new developments in crime fighting. Like a snowball rolling down a hill, forensic science grew, slowly at first but steadily picking

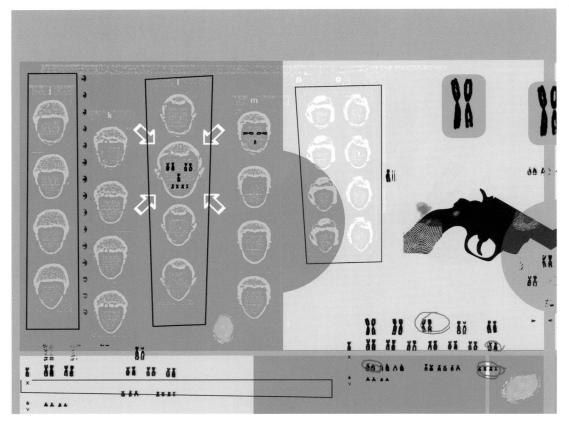

Advances in technology and communication have impacted the growth of forensics.

up speed. A major landmark in forensic science, the discovery that all people have unique fingerprints, denotes the beginning of the current age of crime fighting.

Forensic science has grown rapidly in recent years, expanding as new techniques are developed and new sorts of crimes spread. The ability of people to travel around the world with ease has increased pressure on the forensic community to evolve and adapt. Eyewitnesses are no longer the only way to catch a criminal. Modern forensic science actually refers to the sum of the efforts of many different specialized technicians, each working on a very specific evidence type. Gone are the days of Sherlock Holmes, the fictional English super detective made famous for his use of a wide range of forensic techniques. The professional forensic scientist of the twenty-first century is merely one link in a long chain that handles and examines physical evidence.

2

PHYSICAL EVIDENCE

Imagine this scene: late on a rainy night, a man wearing a knit, black ski mask and dark clothing walks through a yard and approaches the back of a dark house; the only glimpse of skin is his hands. He steps through a flower garden and onto the back patio, stepping softly up to the locked back door. After testing the knob, he breaks in, using a long metal pry bar to rip open the back door. Then he takes out a small flashlight and begins to walk around the dark house, looking for small valuable items that he can easily carry out. He picks up a few things and inspects them, decides that they are not worth the time, and moves on; since he is on foot, the types of valuables he can take are limited. He continues to search, eventually finding a small jewelry box. Jackpot! He breaks open the box and empties the contents into his pocket, then turns and exits the house, running off into the dark, rainy night.

Around the world, hundreds of break-ins like this take place every night. The evidence is often hard to spot—but to a trained crime investigator, it is abundant. Think about the scene described above.

The burglar obviously thought about eyewitnesses, as he was wearing a ski mask. He knew that if a person saw him, he would probably get caught. By wearing the mask, he could avoid being easily identified by anyone who might pass by or glance out a window.

Thieves like this, however, are rarely thorough enough to avoid leaving some evidence behind, traces and marks that can be read by skilled forensic scientists. Read the scenario again. Can you spot the mistakes the thief made?

First, the thief was not wearing gloves; fingerprints are extremely valuable evidence, and he left his on the doorknob and on each item he picked up and examined. Second, he wore a knit mask, likely to shed fibers all over the house. Third, he broke in using a pry bar, an item forensic scientists can trace. He stepped in the flowerbed, no doubt leaving behind the imprint of his shoes since it was a damp night. When the burglar went home, he may have still carried traces of mud on his shoes and might have tracked the dirt around his apartment. If investigators follow the trail of evidence to the burglar's home, that dirt can be the piece of evidence that links the criminal to the crime scene.

Criminals do not always carefully think through their crimes, and those who do rarely take enough steps to prevent evidence transfer during the crime. Crime fighters count on being able to find some form of evidence. In almost all crimes, evidence is everywhere; you just have to know where to look. The basic principle of forensic science, the theory of transfer, holds that each and every physical contact a person has with any surface results in the transfer of some physical material.

An individual who breaks and enters is often unaware of the amount of evidence he leaves at a crime scene.

Nearly every crime scene is full of clues. When a criminal touches something at the scene, chances are he will leave behind some sort of physical evidence, such as a fingerprint, hairs or fibers, dirt from his shoes, or possibly even flecks of paint. Anything left behind as a result of physical contact can be useful in solving a crime. Ballistics—the examination of firearms and the bullets they fire—and ***tool marks*** are also important sources of physical evidence that are commonly found at crime scenes. (A less common but

Physical Evidence   **23**

Case Study:
The Atlanta, Georgia, Murders

Between 1979 and 1981, more than twenty-five black males were killed in the area around Atlanta, Georgia. Investigators had few leads in the case. The only clue linking the killings was that investigators had found similar fibers and what appeared to be dog hairs on many of the bodies. At the state crime laboratory, a criminalist discovered that the fibers were all made of the same type of material, one commonly used in carpets. The finding was leaked to the media, and the evening news reported the discovery.

Soon after the media report, the police began finding bodies stripped and dumped in a local river. The killer apparently watched the news. Police decided to set up a stakeout of the river that was favored by the killer. A number of officers were deployed to monitor the Chattahoochee River in hopes of catching a killer.

The stakeout paid off. Late one night, a pair of officers on patrol heard a loud splash. A white station wagon drove away, crossing a bridge over the river. The vehicle was found and stopped by other officers a few minutes later. The driver, Wayne Williams, claimed he had dumped trash off the bridge. Police were forced to let him go when they could not find anything in the water.

A few days later, the body of twenty-seven-year-old Nathaniel Cater washed ashore downstream of the bridge where Williams had stopped. A single yellow-green fiber, matching the fibers taken from the other bodies, was found caught in his hair. A judge issued a warrant to search Williams' home.

Police investigators entered the house and immediately took notice of the carpet. Yellow-green wall-to-wall carpeting covered the floor. A dog greeted them as they came into the house. Examination of the fibers from the carpet in Williams' house revealed that the fibers were consistent with those found on the bodies. In addition to the carpet fibers from the house, investigators found that a fiber taken from one of the bodies matched the carpet in Williams' white station wagon. The evidence was mounting against him.

Williams was tried for and found guilty of the murders of two of the victims. He was sentenced to two life sentences. Despite Williams' conviction for only two of the murders, the Atlanta police considered twenty-one of the cases closed with this guilty verdict, based largely on trace evidence.

no less important source of physical evidence is any handwriting or typed documents found at the crime scene.)

There are so many different types of physical evidence that it would be nearly impossible to list them all; each crime scene is unique. Criminalists are especially good at recognizing and collecting these varied bits of evidence; they must be ready and willing to adapt and be creative in order to handle the challenges of each scene on an independent basis. No two crime scenes are alike, so the techniques that work at one scene may not work at the next; criminalists must be flexible and innovative while search-

Criminalists discover fiber evidence at a crime scene.

ing for evidence. A skilled investigator may collect more than thirty different pieces of physical evidence from a crime scene.

So, what is the point of collecting all this evidence? The physical evidence found at a crime scene can be used to reconstruct the events that occurred, providing information to jurors hearing the case. Juries often give more weight to evidence that can be conclusively linked to a particular act at a crime scene. For example, evidence collectors often find fibers at a crime scene; if a criminalist can match them to an item known to have been in the possession of the suspect, a link can be made between that suspect and the scene. This can add to the importance of other kinds of evidence gathered at the scene.

Identification

In general, physical evidence is used to provide hints to the identity of the person who committed the crime. This evidence does not always provide a direct link to a suspect. In all cases, however, identification of each piece of evidence is important. For each type of evidence, there is usually a standard method of examination that helps improve the level of acceptance

Along with the marks left on a bullet by the patterns of grooves and ridges in the barrel of a gun, each shell fired is marked by the gun's firing mechanism. The powder used in the shell is an important source of evidence, since guns are often used in crimes. Each bullet manufacturer uses a slightly different formula in its ammunition. Many states maintain databases of the chemical compositions of different gunpowders used by the various ammunition makers. Linking a specific gun to a specific crime is often thought of as the holy grail of crime fighting. Matching gunpowder residue to the gun can be the key to this linkage.

of the evidence in court. In addition, every piece of evidence that can be used to link an individual to a crime scene can and should be used to reduce the amount of uncertainty about the scene itself.

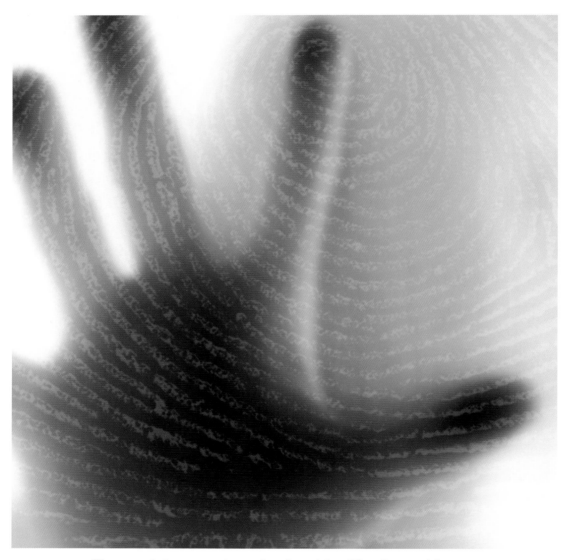

Fingerprints are categorized as identification evidence.

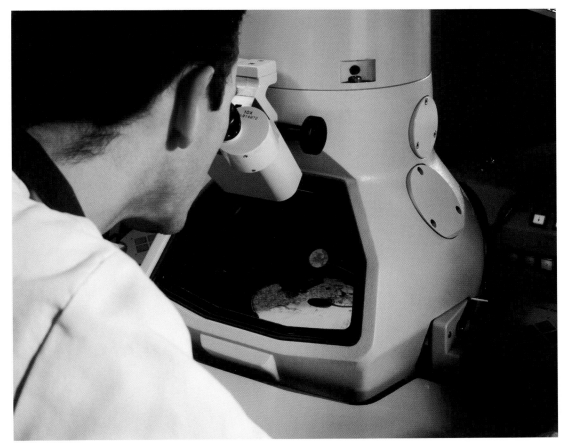

Physical evidence is helpful in recreating the events of a crime.

Physical evidence is not usually the best way to positively identify a criminal. It is more often used to find the evidence that can shed light on the events that occurred before, during, and after the commission of the crime. In terms of solving a crime, physical evidence is most often used to compare a sample taken from the crime scene with one collected during a search and seizure of a suspect's home, car, or other property. Comparison is a very important way to establish the value of a piece of physical evidence.

Evidence with odds like the flip of a coin cannot absolutely link a suspect to a crime.

A sound understanding of statistics is very important to a forensic science expert. Courts often require that a specific evidence type meet very high statistical standards before it can be allowed to prove identity in court.

Comparison

Physical evidence might be the only way to positively link an item to a crime scene. In forensic science, the term **common origin** is often used when examining physical evidence. Determination of common origin relies on an examiner being able to use several analytical tests to identify the properties of the piece of evidence. The forensic scientist must be flexible and creative in her examination. If a sample found at a crime scene can be matched to a sample taken from a suspect, common origin can be established, and the suspect will have some explaining to do. This sort of link is usually vital during criminal trials.

Often a forensic researcher examining a piece of evidence is unable to identify enough properties to make an accurate match to another sample. In these cases, even though a positive match cannot be made, the *probability* of a positive match can be a critical aspect in the usefulness of the piece of evidence in court.

Imagine flipping a coin. Everyone knows that a flipped coin will land either heads up or tails up; there is a 50 percent chance of either outcome. In other words, a person flipping the same coin one hundred times would expect heads to come up fifty times. Evidence with odds like the flip of a coin is not very compelling or useful. Imagine an evidence collector has found a hair at a crime scene. This hair type is common in about two out of every one hundred individuals. Would this be valuable as the only link between a suspect and a crime? Probably not.

Individual Characteristics

Probability is extremely important in determining the source of physical evidence. Sometimes the evidence can be attributed to a specific source with great certainty.

For example, Victor Balthazard, a French scientist, calculated the probability of any two people having the exact same fingerprint as approximately one in 1,000,000,000,000,000,000,000,000,000,000,000,000,000,000,000,000,000,000,000,000,000. Over the course of one hundred years of fingerprint record keeping, there has never been a documented case of two people having the same fingerprint, despite the fact that millions of fingerprints have been examined over that period of time. Because fingerprints are considered such a good way to identify an individual, they are classified as individual characteristics.

Any evidence that can be attributed to a single source with little doubt is called individual evidence, and it carries great weight in the courts. When a jury sees that the odds of two people sharing the same fingerprint are as low as they are, the evidential value of a fingerprint found at a crime scene becomes very high indeed!

In 1903, the New York State prison system began the first systematic use of fingerprints for identification in the United States.

Class Characteristics

On the flip side of the coin is evidence with class characteristics. Class evidence can only be accurately associated with a group of sources, meaning it can never be used to positively identify a single person or source. Blood types, for example, are class evidence because thousands or even millions of people in the world share a common blood type. Type O blood is the most common blood type in the world; 45 percent of all people have this type of blood. These are not good odds for positively identifying a specific person as the source of blood evidence. Additional factors in human blood are often used to increase these odds, but unless DNA evidence is used, blood is not a very good way to identify a person.

Think for a moment about the O. J. Simpson murder trial. At the crime scene, two bodies were found, along with a significant amount of blood. The police quickly identified O. J., a former football hero and the ex-husband of one of the victims, as a prime suspect because of the circumstances of his relationship with his wife and his behavior immediately following the crime. Forensic researchers were able to determine that one of the blood samples found at the scene was type A, a match to O. J.'s blood type. It soon became clear that the blood evidence would be the key to the prosecution's case. Forensic serologists were able to identify three additional factors in the blood that reduced the number of people in the world from whom the sample could have come to less than 0.05 percent, but that was not enough for the jury. DNA evidence was in its infancy and was not particularly well accepted by courts or jurors. In the end, the defense team was able to create enough doubt that the blood came from O. J. that the jury found him not guilty of the charges. O. J. walked away a free man, despite the large body of circumstantial evidence against him.

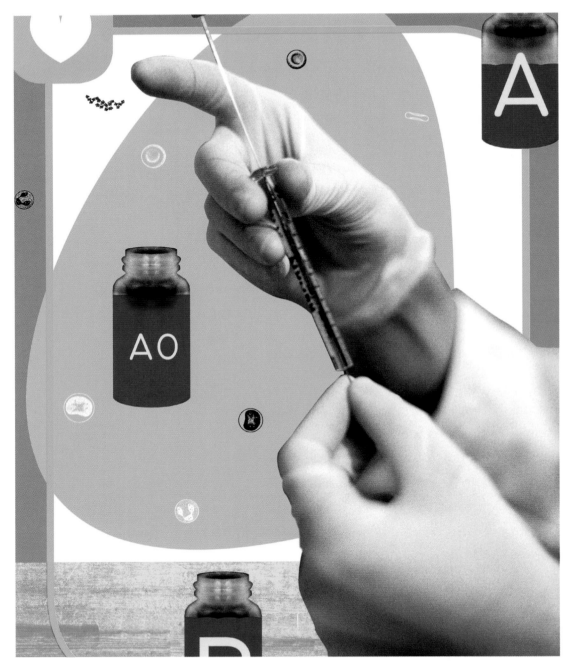

Blood type is more often used to rule out a suspect.

Class evidence can be used to effectively rule out a source or individual in some cases. In the O. J. case, only suspects with type A blood could be linked to the crime scene. Individuals with any of the other three major blood types could effectively be excluded from suspicion because their blood type was not found at the scene.

Crime-Scene Reconstruction

Perhaps the most valuable aspect of physical evidence is in reconstructing events that occurred during the commission of a crime. Each bit of physical evidence tells a story, and a skilled criminalist can interpret the signs and make educated guesses as to what happened. Crime-scene schematics, or drawings, are a common part of court proceedings. Prosecutors and de-

Developments in forensic science, and biological science in general, have exposed many identifying features of blood that are forensically useful. Perhaps most important is the use of DNA found in specific cells within the blood. A relatively rapid procedure can be used to remove and analyze DNA, providing forensic biologists with a very specific genetic profile of the individual whose blood they are examining. DNA evidence can be amazingly specific. It is not uncommon for a forensic biologist to be able to produce statistics that indicate the sample could only have come from 1 in 3 billion people. Few attorneys can argue against that kind of statistical certainty.

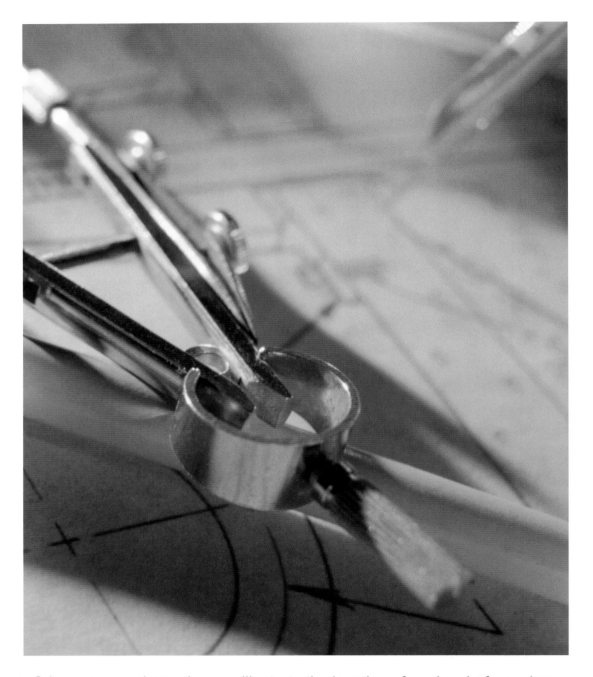

Crime-scene schematics can illustrate the location of a crime before a jury.

MARK & TRACE ANALYSIS

Crime-scene reconstruction is an art form. Prosecutors have been known to hire artists and contractors to build models of the crime scene, scaled down to a size that is useful in a courtroom. Detailed crime-scene reconstructions have been cited by jurors as a major factor in their deliberations, because good visual aids help shape people's thinking.

fense lawyers know the value of a good crime-scene reconstruction in swaying a jury. Visuals, such as a map of the scene, are often a good way to tie together all of the events of the crime. When jurors can actually see what the criminalist thinks happened at the scene, they can give more weight to the small bits of physical evidence he has collected.

The first step in reconstructing a crime scene is to draw sketches of the entire area. To facilitate accurate and comprehensive analysis of a crime scene, it is usually divided into grids. The grids that are laid out should be included in the drawings, so that whoever looks at the sketches can determine exactly where a piece of evidence was found. A piece of evidence that was not properly tagged and stored is often not admissible in court, so the labeling step during collection is very important. If the location of a piece of evidence at the crime scene was not recorded, it cannot be placed on the drawings, and it is not particularly useful in court.

Drawings are usually checked for accuracy by comparing them with photographs taken of the crime scene. Sketches are rarely inaccurate, but

Investigators take careful measurements and notes of the crime scene.

MARK & TRACE ANALYSIS

mistakes do happen from time to time. Usually, this can be corrected by comparison with the photographs, and little damage is done to the body of evidence in the case; that's the reason for taking the pictures, after all. **Redundancy** is very important to forensic scientists and evidence collectors.

After the sketches and photographs have been compared and the scene has been verified, the evidence collectors or criminalists working the case can begin indicating where each piece of evidence was collected. The evidence must be placed as precisely as possible, and additional information about the evidence is often recorded on the drawings as well. Patterns of blood spatter, for example, can provide valuable clues about the amount of force used and the direction from which that force came. Glass fragments around a window may help determine the direction of travel of whatever

Crime-scene reconstruction is a valuable way to examine the evidence and determine how each piece relates to the crime. After looking at the sketches and comparing the evidence to what she thinks happened, it is not uncommon for a specialist to determine that some item found at the crime scene is not at all related to the crime. Excluding false evidence can save thousands of dollars for the forensic laboratory and many hours of a criminalist's time. When there are hundreds of bits of evidence to examine, this can be very important. Crime laboratories operate under tight budgets, so saving money and time is vital.

Photographs taken at a crime scene can be more accurate than sketches.

broke the glass. The positions of fingerprints can even be used to make conclusions about the height of the person who left them. Each of these pieces of physical evidence provides important clues that help solve the crime.

Evidence collection units (ECUs) find and collect various pieces of evidence—the traces and marks—at crime scenes. Evidence must be handled very carefully, and according to specific rules of evidence. In forensic science, the **chain of custody** is among the most important parts of evidence handling. Typically, a signature must be provided each time the evidence passes from person to person. A record of who handled evidence and why each person needed it can be vital to maintaining the value of the evidence in court. The ECU investigating a crime scene carefully logs each piece of evidence and then ships the entire collection to a crime laboratory, where it is examined one piece at a time.

The chain of custody is perhaps the most controversial aspect of evidence collection. For example, many people feel the outcome of the O.J. Simpson trial hinged on the failure of the police and ECU to fully maintain the chain of custody. Vials of blood went missing, only to turn up later in the possession of one of the inspectors on the case. This allowed defense attorneys to shed doubt on the value of the blood evidence found at the crime scene and in the suspect's bedroom.

Organization of a
Typical Crime Laboratory

Crime laboratories around the country are typically divided into several different departments. One reason for this separation is that it is far easier to maintain the different types of evidence in specialized departments that have been set up to handle a narrow range of evidence types. In addition, each lab is staffed by specialists who are highly trained to examine the specific evidence type of that particular laboratory. The equipment in each lab is, by nature, specialized, and the commonly accepted methods for evidence examination do not allow for the sharing of equipment between labs. In fact, it is not uncommon for a given piece of equipment to be certified only for use within one specific forensic laboratory.

As with almost every aspect of forensic science, separating the individual departments within a crime laboratory is done with a nod to the courts. Splitting the crime laboratory into many smaller departments ensures that each piece of evidence is less likely to be contaminated by contact with other evidence. Properly maintaining the delicate equipment of different departments is also easier if it is used only by specifically trained individuals. Specific technicians in each section of the crime laboratory are responsible for cleaning and *calibrating* the equipment in their section.

Every state in the United States has at least one full-service forensic laboratory. (In Canada, most police departments take advantage of the Royal Canadian Mounted Police crime labs in Vancouver, Ottawa, and Edmonton.) In order to be considered full service, a crime laboratory should include each of the following departments:

Who, when, and why someone handles evidence is strictly monitored.

Members of the ECU are also known as crime-scene analysts (CSAs) in some regions of the United States. The title varies by state, but in truth, they are one and the same. Each is responsible for finding and collecting the evidence at the scene of a crime.

A successful analysis relies on the ability of the ECU to work methodically and to thoroughly examine every inch of a crime scene using a variety of collection techniques. When evidence is particularly hard to come by, the ECU often turns to less standard methods, because the collection of evidence is usually far less scrutinized than evidence examination is.

- ECU
- physical science unit
- biology unit
- firearms and ballistics unit
- photography unit
- identification unit
- evidence storage unit

Each individual unit handles very specific evidence types. The biology unit, for example, would process any blood evidence collected by the ECU. The specific equipment found in each unit of a crime laboratory

A broken window may hold valuable clues to the events of a crime.

CASE STUDY: RESPONSIBILITIES OF THE FORENSIC SCIENTIST

On April 19, 1995, the Murrah Federal Building in Oklahoma City, Oklahoma, was bombed in a terrorist attack. Timothy McVeigh and Terry Nichols detonated a truck bomb outside of the building, killing 168 people, many of them children attending a day-care center. Although McVeigh and Nichols went to trial as the sole perpetrators of the crime, some of the evidence pointed to a third person behind the bombing. When defense attorneys discovered an unaccounted-for leg among the remains found in the rubble, they were convinced that this was a piece of the missing bomber—a piece that could solve the puzzle and help the defense's case.

The leg, amputated just above the knee, was dressed in the remains of military fatigues, a dark sock, and a combat boot. Could it be the leg of a terrorist in militia garb? Plastic shards from the bomb seemed to show its owner had been near the center of the blast. The leg was assumed to be a man's because of its dress and the fact it was unshaven, with dark, curly hair. The skin appeared light but was in a state of advanced decomposition.

The FBI called in a forensic anthropologist to study the leg. The notch of the knee joint showed that its owner was black. Investigation showed that the leg belonged to a woman. Even further investigation identified her as Airman First Class Lakesha Levy, a twenty-one-year-old service woman with the U.S. Air Force, killed while applying for a Social Security card and buried with the wrong leg. This second "wrong leg" turned out to belong to a white female—and investigators have still not found a third bomber.

varies depending on that unit's needs. Together, the units work to analyze the traces and marks left behind by criminals. The smallest fiber, the tiniest hair, the most infinitesimal speck of dirt may have an important story to tell.

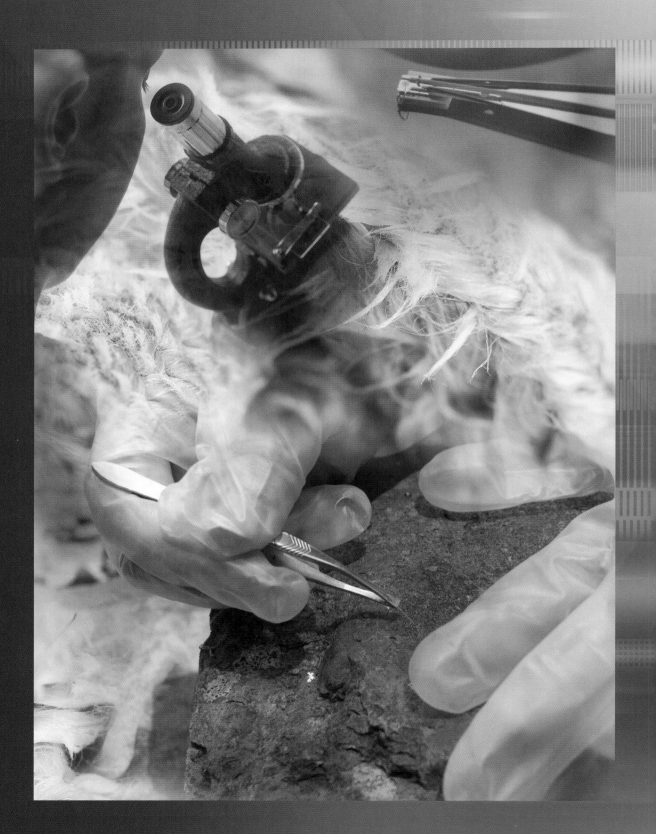

3

TRACE EVIDENCE THAT LEADS TO CONVICTIONS

In 1982, a girl was kidnapped from a baseball field near her home in Ohio. Her body was found approximately thirty miles away (48.3 kilometers). She had been strangled.

Investigators found a number of orange polyester fibers in her hair. The fibers had a unique shape, and a criminalist examining them believed they might have come from a carpet. In addition, a cardboard box and plastic wrap were found near the body. The box had been used to ship a bench seat for a box van. Police began working that lead.

A short time later, an Ohio woman was kidnapped from a nearby park. The kidnapper took her to his home, where he held her hostage for a short time. When he left to get food, she escaped. She was able to lead police to his house, where they found a white box van. In the van was a bench seat like the one shipped in the box found near the earlier body. What's more, the floor of the van was covered in orange carpeting. Fibers pulled from the van's floor proved to be a match for those found on the body.

In order to build the strongest case possible, investigators traced the fabric of the carpet to one specific supplier. Only seventy-four yards (22.3 meters) of that particular color carpet were sold in Ohio in the years before the killing. Once the case was fully established, police closed their net on Robert Anthony Buell. Buell was convicted of the murder of the eleven-year-old girl and pleaded no contest to charges surrounding the kidnapping and rape of the Ohio woman as well as that of a West Virginia woman. He was sentenced to 121 years in prison for the crimes against the women, and he was executed on September 24, 2002, for the strangulation of the little girl.

It may seem like trace evidence is not a terribly useful sort of evidence. How can such tiny pieces of material be a valuable source of information about a crime? To a criminalist, however, trace evidence is a gold mine. Wherever a criminal goes, she leaves behind something, regardless of how

Trace evidence can be so small that it is invisible to the naked eye. This does not stop the forensic expert from using it to add to the information about the case. Often, it is necessary to use a microscope to find tiny fragments of glass or fiber that might be around the crime scene. An effective way to gather trace evidence of the smallest size is to vacuum the area. A clean vacuum bag and a slow hand can gather enough dust and fiber evidence to keep a trace expert busy for weeks.

hard she tries to clean up. Blood can be washed and fingerprints wiped away, but something is always left behind that she fails to notice. It is the presence of these unseen pieces of trace evidence that a wise criminalist looks for and then uses to link a person to the crime scene.

Evidence Types Commonly Found in Trace Amounts

Just about anything can be considered trace evidence as long as it is found in very small quantities. Hairs, fibers, flecks of paint, tiny slivers of wood or other plant material, and soil are all commonly found in trace amounts at crime scenes. In general, the most common trace evidence at a crime scene is hair and fibers. Criminals rarely commit crimes totally naked (though it does happen from time to time), and clothing is constantly shedding over the course of its life.

To test this, get a piece of tape and find an area of the floor that looks clean. Place the sticky side of the tape down against the floor and lift it back up slowly. Take a look at the tape now. In most indoor areas, a simple tape lift like this will reveal hundreds of bits of material that can be used as evidence.

Each fragment of a person's clothing can be very informative. Think about this scenario: a woman with blond hair enters a convenience store with her back to the surveillance camera. She is wearing dark clothing and carrying a gun. After taking the cash from the register, she shoots and kills the clerk, the sole witness to the robbery. She runs out the door and down the street to her car, where she quickly changes her clothes before driving away. After a few miles, she pulls over and tosses the gun into a deep river, sure that it will not be easily found, then continues driving.

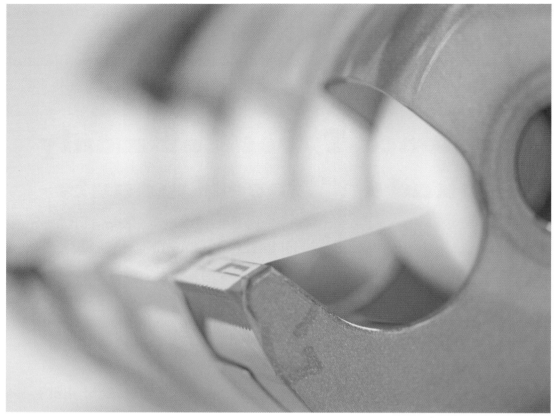

A simple piece of tape can lift telling evidence from the scene of a crime.

A few miles down the road, a police officer is parked, clocking the speeds of oncoming traffic. A car speeds by and is clocked at twelve miles (19.3 kilometers) over the speed limit. He calls in to his station and sets out after the car. In the heat of the moment, the woman tries to escape. A high-speed chase ensues, and she is eventually caught and arrested.

At the **impound** yard, the inspector notices a pile of dark clothing in the backseat and marks it in his log book. At about the same time, investigators at the convenience store find dark fibers on the floor and countertop near the register. They determine that the fibers do not match the dead clerk's clothing and log them as evidence.

A few hours later, the investigators cross-reference the evidence they have collected with the traffic stops for the night and notice that a car with a pile of dark clothing in the backseat has been impounded. In the face of this development, a judge quickly authorizes a search of the car. The

Trace evidence can be more compelling than what is caught on video surveillance.

Trace Evidence That Leads to Convictions

CASE STUDY:
A TELL-TALE HAIR

In Telluride, Colorado, in 1990, a woman found her mother dead on the floor of her home. A single gunshot wound to the head was the cause of death. At first, the victim's husband was the primary suspect, but investigators ruled him out as the killer. He had no motive for killing his wife, no history of violent behavior, and he appeared honestly distraught over her death; eventually, he was cleared of suspicion. The police had evidence they felt would allow them to break the case quickly, but this was not to be.

The killing went unsolved for several years, even though police had good ballistics evidence. All they needed to do was find that gun. Three years later, a man in Nevada called Telluride police to say that he thought his brother, Frank Marquis, had committed the crime; Marquis had apparently confessed at a party. Police attempted to get a taped confession using a phone tap but were unsuccessful. A judge granted the investigators a warrant to search Marquis's home, where they found a gun that matched the type used to kill the Colorado woman. The barrel had been gouged deeply with a tool, perhaps a screwdriver, changing the ballistic marks made on a test bullet fired by the gun. The police would need to find other evidence.

Police were able to trace Marquis's movements to Colorado the weekend of the killing. The investigators then found the man who traveled with Marquis from Nevada to Colorado that weekend. On questioning, they discovered that the man had not remained in Marquis's company the entire weekend. On the drive back to Nevada, his companion reported that Marquis had thrown two packages out the car window. Police believed this to be the clothing he had worn during the killing.

Scouring the roadways between the two states, the police were amazed to find two bundles of clothing buried under piles of dirt from roadway construction. A criminalist found a single strand of blond hair, a close match to the hair of the deceased. In addition, there was plenty of hair that matched Marquis's. Workers within the crime lab were able to provide the evidence that led to Marquis's arrest.

After learning of the discovery of the clothing, Marquis confessed. He swore it was a botched burglary and that everything went horribly wrong when the woman caught him in the act. He was convicted of manslaughter and sentenced to twenty-four years in prison.The United States Federal Bureau of Investigation (FBI) maintains a handbook of forensic methods and techniques for use by all states in the country. Most state crime laboratories refer to this work as the definitive standard for the analysis of evidence. In the handbook, there are hundreds of different techniques and guidelines for their usage.

investigators examine the clothing and are able to match the fibers. The woman can now be listed as an official suspect in the killing. Investigators find gunpowder residue on the back of her right hand, which they are able to match to the type of powder used in the bullet that caused the death of the clerk, since he was shot at close range, leaving powder burns on his clothing.

The woman insists she is innocent of the killing, claiming she had been at the crime scene to buy a drink a few minutes before the killing. The evidence against her does not include the murder weapon, but the trace evidence collected clearly links her to the scene. Prosecutors are able to easily connect her to the crime scene and the shooting, and she is sentenced to prison for life, based largely on the trace evidence collected by the skilled criminalists working the case.

Collecting Trace Evidence

Once the police have secured the crime scene, the ECU begins its work. Evidence collectors systematically search the area, taking photographs and drawing detailed sketches as they go. After the entire area is photographed, the ECU typically divides the scene into a grid (like graph paper) and works one square at a time, from the outermost squares toward the center. They work slowly but steadily through the entire area in this way. It is not uncommon for the process to take a full week to complete.

Trace evidence can pose some very specific problems for investigators because it is by nature very small in quantity and size. A single hair can be critical evidence if it can be used to link a person to a crime scene. Each type of trace evidence is collected differently, meaning that a forensic criminalist or evidence collector must have a relatively deep bag of collection tricks at his disposal.

The typical light source used by the ECU can be set to a variety of wavelengths, so one lamp is all that is needed to look for a wide variety of different materials. In addition, special filters can be attached that change the characteristics of the light cast by the lamp, further expanding the spectrum of materials that can be found with one light source.

For hairs and fibers, a method called a tape lift is often the best way to gather the evidence. One of the best tools for hair and fiber collection is a lint roller, commercially available at stores around the country. Lint rollers are essentially rolls of tape with the sticky side facing outward. Simply rolling the tool across the surface picks up hairs and fibers. After each pass, the outer layer of tape can be removed, and labeled with the identification number from the grid, and placed in a plastic bag to be sent to the crime laboratory.

A magnifying glass and forceps (more commonly known as tweezers) are standard tools for the collection of pieces of glass, paint flecks, slivers of wood, and other bits of evidence that can be picked up from surfaces. By carefully examining every square inch in the evidence collection grid, an evidence collector can maximize the amount of evidence he finds.

Alternative light sources are commonly used for revealing hidden pieces of trace evidence. Sometimes, this evidence goes unnoticed until the ECU shines light of a specific wavelength on it. Ultraviolet light and low-power lasers are very useful when trying to find tiny threads or hairs, glass, and even spots of blood. The ECU team members know that light of different wavelengths will react with many of the materials they commonly find at a crime scene, allowing them to spot even the tiniest pieces of evidence.

Trace Evidence Analysis

How does a criminalist go about the business of examining all the different bits of evidence collected from a typical crime scene? The answer is: very carefully and methodically. As with most other types of forensically valuable evidence, trace evidence is treated with great care. Courtroom rules are usually the most important factors forensic scientists consider when they develop methods for examining a piece of evidence, and *standardized* methods are usually the rule. Trace evidence is a special case,

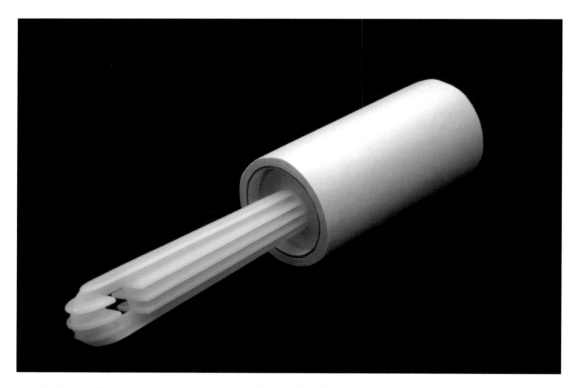

A lint roller is an important tool in collecting potential forensic samples.

however, and often methods must be modified to gather information. Trace evidence comes from a wide variety of sources, so the methods for examining it must be just as varied.

Trace examination can be surprisingly time consuming and complicated. Take the examination of hairs found at a crime scene as an example. The typical examination of hairs or fibers starts with a microscopic examination under normal white light.

The cuticle of a hair, or the outer shell, is often very different from person to person, and sometimes it is different on hairs from different parts of the body. The cuticle usually looks scaly, like the skin of a fish; the scales tend to be organized in patterns that can be compared. There are three major types of scale appearances for most hairs: coronal, spinous, and imbricate. Coronal scales look like tiny crowns wrapped around the shaft of the hair. Human hairs rarely have coronal scales on the cuticle. Spinous scales are kite shaped, with a sharp looking point on each scale. This type of scale is also rare in humans; cats are the most common source of hairs with spinous cuticle scales. Imbricate scales are flattened, like pancakes, and layered upon each other. This is the most common type of cuticle scale found in human hairs because of the way the hair grows. Imbricate scales are also found on the hairs of many other mammals, so scale type is not always a good way to identify a source. Scale type is most often used to weed out the noninformative hairs gathered at a crime scene, such as those from the family cat or the mouse that lives in the baseboard.

The largest part of a human hair is called the cortex, where the pigment (which determines hair color) is located. A criminalist looks at the cortex for patterns in the pigmentation, because most of the time, two hairs from the same region of a person's body will have very similar pigment patterns. Sometimes, the cortex of a hair allows a criminalist to make an educated guess as to the race of the person whose hair she is examining.

Trace Evidence That Leads to Convictions   59

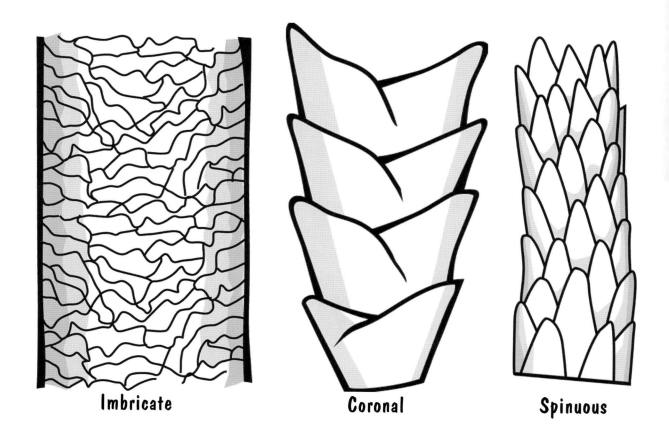

| Imbricate | Coronal | Spinuous |

Imbricate, coronal, and spinous scales on hair.

At the center of a hair is a central shaft called the medulla. Often resembling an empty tube, the width of the medulla is proportional to the diameter of the shaft of the hair. Surprisingly, the width of the medulla can be an informative bit of data. This is measured as a figure called the medullary index. In most animals, the medullary index is 0.5 or greater, meaning that the medulla is at least half as thick as the diameter of the entire hair.

Every state in the United States maintains its own database of hair characteristics. In general, the databases are used to rule out evidence rather than identify individuals that might have left the evidence. Since hair evidence is so commonly found at crime scenes, it is very useful to have the capability to rule out any hairs that might have been left by an animal unconnected with the crime.

In humans, the medullary index is usually less than 0.3, about one-third the diameter of the hair itself. Patterns found in the medulla are useful to criminalists. Different animals have different medulla patterns, allowing a researcher to determine from what species a particular hair came.

Fibers can be compared in much the same way as hairs, with a few notable differences. Since fibers can be either natural or synthetic, they tend to be more variable than hairs. The main differences from one fiber to the next are usually seen in the outer edges of the fiber under normal white light. Some fibers have smooth, tight outer shells, whereas others have rough or loose edges. Nylon, for example, is a synthetic fiber that tends to be relatively smooth as a result of how it is made. Cotton and wool, however, often look quite hairy when viewed through a microscope. Worldwide, cotton is the fiber found most often at crime scenes because of its use in clothing.

In general, the physical appearance of a fiber or hair can be accurately characterized by simply looking at it closely. Sometimes, however, simple observation will not do the trick, and a criminalist has to reach further into his bag of tricks to see the differences. On *CSI*, the investigators almost always use a bluish light to examine different surfaces. Called an ultraviolet (UV) lamp, it is one example of an alternate light source. Because the light reacts differently with some substances than others, it sometimes reveals hidden details about the crime scene. Criminalists often use these light sources in conjunction with a microscope to examine the surfaces of a hair or fiber more closely, hoping to gather more information about the particular fiber than they could under white light. If you have ever stood under a black light, you will recall that every bit of light fabric you wore seemed to glow brightly; darker colors looked almost black. The same sort of reaction

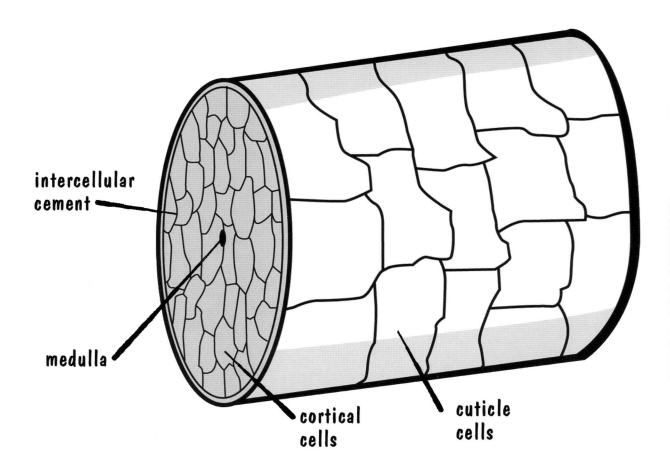

Diagram of the components of hair.

occurs when a criminalist examines a fiber with UV light. In fact, the black lights sold at most stores are simply less powerful versions of the same light used in forensic situations. A criminalist using UV light and a microscope often can see details in the material she is studying that were not visible under white light.

The properties of light are used to examine the structure of many types of evidence found in trace amounts. Light travels away from the source in waves, and any object it strikes reflects a portion of the light wave. The colors that are visible are actually the reflected light bouncing off the ob-

Medulla patterns found on a strand of hair.

Trace Evidence That Leads to Convictions

Because cotton fabric is made from natural fibers, traces of cotton at crime scenes are easily identifiable.

Alternate light sources can reveal details about a fiber that white light cannot.

ject. People can only see a very small part of the total spectrum of light, but machines have been developed that can be used to examine light in much greater detail. A special machine called a spectrophotometer can be used to analyze the colors of a piece of evidence. A close look at an item that appears blue may reveal that it is in fact a blend of many colors. The spectrophotometer can detect the slightest difference in color between two objects. This is invaluable to the criminalist examining a paint chip or a colored fiber. It can mean the difference between the evidence being categorized as class or individual. If the criminalist is able to find enough characteristics that are specific to that particular piece of evidence, then he might be able to assign a specific identity to it.

In addition to the spectrophotometer, another special instrument, the Fourier-Transform Infrared Spectroscope (FTIR), can be used to examine the spectrum of colors found in a particular sample, providing characteristics that can be matched to other samples. Each item examined with FTIR

Ultraviolet light will cause otherwise unseen fluids to fluoresce.

A spectrophotometer can detect slight differences in color between two objects.

Trace Evidence That Leads to Convictions

In the 1980s, a slew of complaints against the baby food giant Gerber came in advance of a series of lawsuits. A number of consumers reported that they had found pieces of glass in jars of baby food they had purchased. Forensic analysis of the glass showed that it had come from a variety of sources, leading to the belief that the glass was not coming from the Gerber plant. A series of tests proved the glass Gerber used for their baby food jars did not match glass recovered from the jars of the people who filed the complaints. These results indicated that Gerber was not at fault, but that the glass was being placed in the baby food after purchase. In other words, people were trying to get rich. They failed.

imaging typically has a slightly different spectrum of colors, a fact that is forensically important. A comparison of the FTIR spectrums of two different samples can help a criminalist determine whether they came from the same source.

When a criminalist examines physical evidence such as soil or glass, he needs to look at more than just the color. Chemical treatments are often used to determine the properties of the material. Glass, for example, is usually examined to determine its *index of refraction.*

A fragment of glass is placed in a succession of special solutions. Each sheet of glass is slightly different due to variations that arise during manufacturing when glass is produced in large vats and then molded to whatever shape is needed. Slight differences in the amounts of ingredients from one batch to the next can change the chemical and physical properties of the glass, and a skilled criminalist knows how to find these differences.

Glass produced by two different companies may have very different chemical structures and therefore have very different indexes of refraction. Glass can rarely be attributed to a single source because it is typically mass-produced. Therefore, glass is usually thought of as class evidence.

In many cases, criminalists need to identify the exact chemical makeup of a piece of trace evidence. A special machine called a gas chromato-

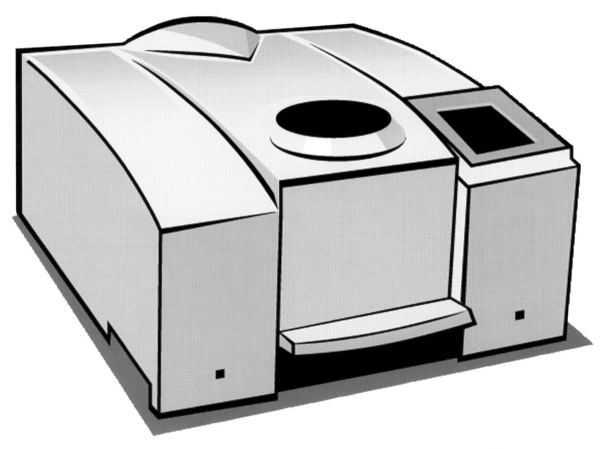

The FTIR examines the spectrum of colors found in a sample.

graph/mass spectrophotometer (GC/MS) is used to examine the chemical composition of evidence. This device can be used to produce a very detailed analysis of the molecules present in the sample. In general, the procedure requires the criminalist to inject a very small amount of liquefied sample into a tiny plastic tube. The sample is drawn into the machine, where the molecules are broken into smaller pieces. The machine outputs a graph that shows the mass of each remaining fragment. The graph is then matched against a database of fragment patterns, allowing the criminalist to positively identify the structure of the evidence.

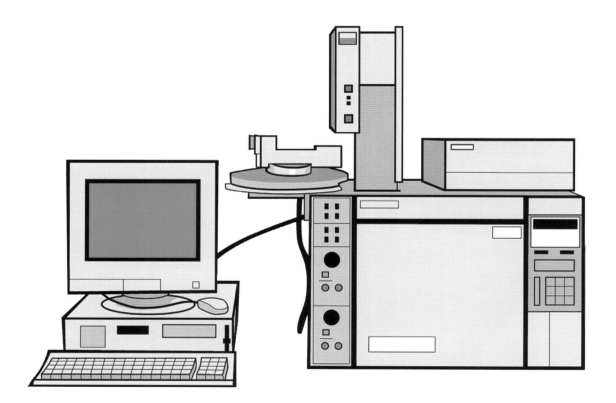

A gas chromatograph.

The GC/MS provides an important way to analyze trace evidence and is a very important piece of laboratory equipment for a criminalist. But crime-solvers have still more in their repertoire, including the clues to be gained from analyzing tool marks.

4

CRACKING CASES WITH TOOL MARKS

On March 1, 1932, Charles and Anne Lindbergh discovered to their horror that their twenty-month-old son had been kidnapped. The kidnapper had climbed up a homemade ladder and entered the nursery through a window some time between 9:00 and 10:00 p.m. The nurse entered the room at about 10 p.m. to check on the baby, and discovered he was missing.

The police were called as soon as the kidnapping was discovered. A ransom of $50,000 was demanded by the kidnapper. The money was paid, but the family was greatly saddened to find that the man who accepted the payment had lied. The baby was not where the man had said he would be once the ransom was paid. Weeks passed, and the baby was not seen.

Seventy-three days later, the body of a baby was found lying under leaves, covered with insects and badly decayed. Charles Lindbergh and the nurse were brought to identify the remains, and they confirmed it was the body of little Charles Jr. The baby had been found.

Three years later, the gold certificates that Charles Lindbergh had used as payment of the ransom began turning up around New York City. Investigators charted the pattern of recovery of the certificates and theorized that the person cashing them lived in or near the Bronx. A breakthrough was made when a gas station attendant reported that a man had paid for gas with one of the certificates. Suspicious, the attendant had written down the man's license plate number.

Charles Lindbergh

Over time, tools develop identifying scratches that can later link them to a crime.

Police traced the license number to Bruno Hauptmann, a German immigrant who matched the descriptions given by the man who had delivered the ransom money and the gas station attendant. Police took him into custody the next day. More than $14,000 in gold certificates were found in his garage; he swore he had found the money. A piece of evidence that proved among the most vital to the case was produced by a U.S. Forest Service worker, who successfully matched the entry marks on the Lindbergh baby's window frame to tools found in Hauptmann's garage. Tool marks on the

Cracking Cases with Tool Marks   **75**

ladder, which had been left at the crime scene, also matched tools belonging to the suspect. Hauptmann was convicted and sentenced to death for the kidnapping and killing of the Lindbergh baby.

The ECU searches for signs of tool usage every time they find signs of a forced entry at a crime scene. Prying open a door with a bar, jimmying a lock with a screwdriver, or unlatching a window lock with a knife blade are all common forms of breaking into locked homes. Each of these methods of foiling a lock leaves behind tell-tale signs. Scratches and gouges left by the tools used to break into a house are often forensically important pieces of evidence. Tools, like people, usually have a sort of "fingerprint."

During the life of a tool, scratches, chips, and dents can alter its surface. Then, when a tool is used to pry open a door, for example, the gouges on the tool leave raised ridges in the wood of the doorframe. Using a comparison microscope, a criminalist can examine the ridges on the wood and match them to marks on the tool. Like a fingerprint, this evidence can be used to positively link a tool to the damage done to the wood during the break-in.

In addition to matching the tool to the method of entry, tool-mark evidence is important to the prosecutor building her case because in most cases, she needs to be able to reconstruct the crime scene. Evidence makes more sense when all the gaps can be filled. Once the method of entry has been established, reconstruction of the events that took place tends to be easier for the investigators; they know where to start looking for evidence. If investigators can establish that the criminal climbed through a window to enter the house, the ECU can tailor their search grid to include the window and the area beneath it outside the house. More evidence is almost always better in forensic cases.

Plaster or latex molds are a very common method of collecting evidence at a crime scene. All manner of evidence that leaves some form of impression can be collected using these two compounds. Many crimes have been solved using impression evidence gathered with plaster. Databases of tire print patterns are being produced by the FBI and many state forensic laboratories, allowing a forensic expert to quickly match a particular impression to a specific manufacturer. While being class evidence, this sort of identification is important because it allows the investigators to rule out millions of potential suspects.

How Do Investigators Collect Tool-Mark Evidence?

Gathering evidence can be very challenging for the ECU. This can be especially true where tool mark evidence has been located. Most often, tool marks are found dug into wood on door casings or window frames. Many houses have metal doors and window frames, however, posing greater challenges. The ECU cannot allow these challenges to stop them from collecting the evidence.

The first step in collecting tool-mark evidence is photographing the damage. A special photography technique called oblique lighting allows the ECU to take pictures that are very detailed, showing location and relative depth of the striations and other grooves left behind by the tool. Simple photography, where the picture is taken from directly above the marks using flat white light from a standard flash, is not sufficient because the im-

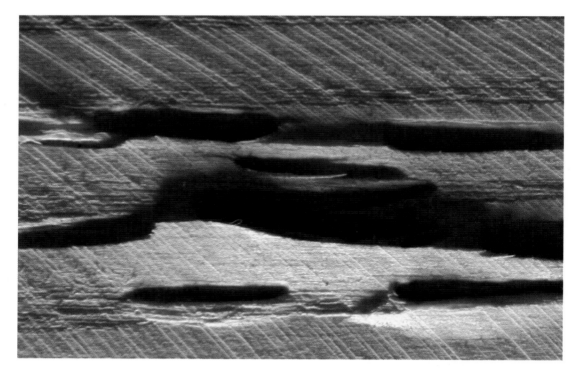

An example of oblique lighting. Notice how you can decipher depth and texture.

age produced will lack depth. Standard pictures are flat two-dimensional images. **Oblique** lighting, where the light source (or sources) is placed above and to the side of the tool mark, illuminates the grooves and ridges in a way that gives viewers an idea of the depth of the grooves and the height of the ridges.

In addition to photography, the ECU can collect tool-mark evidence by making plaster or latex molds of the damage. When properly applied, plaster can be an extremely effective way to examine the details of a tool mark. Latex is used for finer tool marks, where the size of the mark is small, because it captures fine detail with greater accuracy than plaster. Plaster molds are ideal for storing the evidence because once they are formed, they are strong and

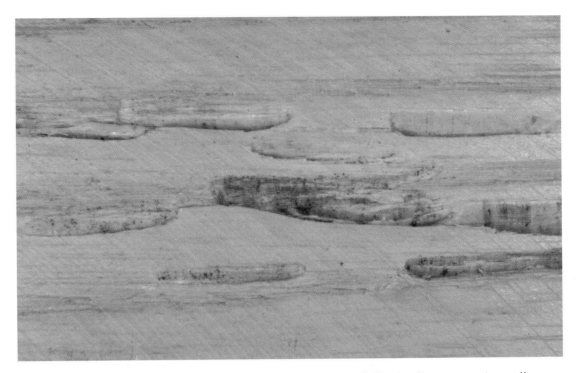

The same shot taken with a white light standard flash. It seems two-dimensional.

durable, and can be safely stored for years. Latex is less durable and prone to tearing because it is a relatively thin, flexible sheet. Plaster or latex molds can be effective pieces of evidence because they can be passed around to jurors during court proceedings, allowing them to take a closer look.

Sometimes making molds is not an option. In these cases, the most common solution is to grab a saw and cut out the section with the tool mark on it. This may seem drastic, but keep in mind that the damaged window or door will likely need replacement anyway—and it is very important to take all measures to solve the crime. A section of wood cut from the frame around a window or door is more valuable than a plaster mold, but it is somewhat less durable in storage.

Matching the Mark to the Tool

When tool marks are discovered, investigators keep their eyes open for tools that might have made them. A suspect's garage full of tools opens a whole new world of possibility for the ECU. It can be a tedious task to examine each tool for the proper patterns, but finding one that matches the marks found at the crime scene can be strong evidence, so it is important

A world of potential evidence lies in a suspect's collection of tools.

to be thorough. Tool-mark matching is done mostly by comparison. The tool is usually collected and entered as evidence, then sent to the crime laboratory for examination by the criminalist working on the case. At the crime lab, the marks on the face of the tool can be compared to the tool marks found at the crime scene. Most often, a comparison microscope is used to examine the pattern of grooves and ridges on the face of the tool. Sometimes, the criminalist uses the tool to gouge a piece of wood or metal to determine whether the tool makes marks that match the evidence collected from the crime scene.

In addition to comparing the marks left by the tool, tiny pieces of metal found in and around the mark at the crime scene can often be matched to the tool. Chemical analysis of the metal can provide more evidence that indicates that the tool, or at least one made by the same manufacturer, was used at the crime scene. GC/MS analysis of the metal can also be used to determine the composition of the tool's metal, and sometimes even identify the manufacturer of the tool since companies often use a specific metal formula with all of their tools; this formula is rarely the same from manufacturer to manufacturer. Identifying where the tool was made is class evidence, but it can still be forensically important. As always, the more evidence the better.

That's one reason forensic science is a growing field. As science makes new discoveries and greater technological advances, criminologists have more and more tasks in their repertoire. What's more, in our post-9/11 world, more and more money is being allocated for domestic security. As a result, many cities are expanding their crime laboratories—and criminology is one of the fastest-growing employment fields.

5

WORKING WITH MARK AND TRACE EVIDENCE

Dian Fossey, the famed naturalist well known for her work with mountain gorillas in Africa, was murdered on December 26, 1985, in her cabin in Rwanda. She had been expecting violence, as a number of threats had been made against her. In the days leading up to her death, her pet parrots were all poisoned. A carved likeness of a puff adder, a deadly African snake, was found on her doorstep; according to African folklore, the puff adder meant she was marked for death. Although Fossey wrote in her journal about receiving threats, she had not paid much attention to them. She did, however, have a handgun near her bed.

Exactly two months after the day she received the carving, someone broke into her cabin through the wall. She lunged for her gun as the person came at her. Two vicious blows to her head, probably with a machete, ended the strug-

Dian Fossey studied gorillas in Rwandan jungles.

gle. She had managed to get the gun, and the ammunition clip was in her left hand as she died. Her aide discovered her body the following morning.

African authorities quickly named two suspects in the case. One was a guide whom Fossey had fired from his post. The other was a student from Oklahoma who was working nearby. Neither person made much sense as a suspect, and the accusations were apparently made to ease the pressure on the Rwandan government following the killing.

In the meantime, informed individuals began to quietly mention that Protais Zigiranyirazo, the brother-in-law of the Rwandan president, had ordered the killing. More commonly known as Mr. Z., he had made millions exploiting the mountain gorillas, and he had been at odds with Fossey for many years as a result of his profits.

The Rwandan government protected Mr. Z. from international authorities until 1994, when an airplane crash took the life of the president. Rwandan authorities quickly determined the crash to be an assassination by the minority Tutsi people of the country. Mr. Z. was instrumental in ordering *genocide* against the Tutsi in response. More than 900,000 Tutsi died in

Fossey's murder may have been linked to Zigiranyirazo's exploitation of mountain gorillas.

Working with Mark and Trace Evidence

the aftermath. Eventually, an outraged international community worked to end the conflict, and Mr. Z. fled the country.

The protections given to Mr. Z. by the Rwandan government were now gone. The evidence against him in the Fossey killing began to pile up, but the investigators would have to wait. He was captured in Belgium in 2001 and charged with war crimes. Solving the murder of Dian Fossey relies largely on fingerprints on both a handwritten document and the murder weapon. Despite this evidence, and the fact that the Rwandan government publicly identifies him as the leader of the Fossey killing, Mr. Z. will probably never face this murder charge. He has served several years in prison for war crimes, but was acquitted in 2009.

Crime labs around the world solve crimes like Mr. Z.'s every day. In each lab, professionals with various jobs work together to find answers. Each position is different, and each has unique requirements.

Among these different positions, the criminalist's job is the most flexible in terms of requirements. Since criminalists are expected to handle a wide variety of evidence, using a wide variety of techniques, the preparation for the job can also be varied. In general, all positions that require handling and examination of evidence require a high level of education. All profes-

Most colleges and universities now offer seminar courses where students in the sciences are required to research a subject and then present their findings to a group of their peers and faculty. These courses are valuable preparation for a career in forensic science because the audience is encouraged to ask questions and debate the points the presenter makes during the presentation.

sional forensic jobs require at least a four-year degree from an accredited college or university. Specific requirements vary from state to state, and it is not uncommon for candidates applying for work to have completed master's degrees or even doctorates.

College Coursework

Prospective criminalists have the distinct advantage of extremely flexible education requirements. A typical college preparatory pathway to working in a forensic laboratory includes a number of varied science classes and as many laboratory sections as possible. The work that goes on in university labs is a great way to prepare for the evidence handling done by a criminalist. Practice is the best way to become comfortable with the many types of delicate instruments commonly used to examine evidence, and laboratory courses offer the opportunity to learn to use many of the more important pieces of equipment.

Forensic biologists, for example, deal solely with biological evidence, but criminalists must work with physics, chemistry, and biology, each of the three major branches of science. Science classes commonly taken by future forensic scientists may include organic chemistry, analytical chemistry, biochemistry, and physics. Each of these courses introduces students to a variety of scientific principles and equipment that are commonly used in forensic laboratories.

Science courses are not the only way to prepare for a career in forensic science. As experts in the field of trace evidence, criminalists are often called as witnesses in court proceedings. A criminalist needs to be able to quickly and clearly explain to an audience, often while under great pressure, how evidence relates to the case and why it is important. Defense attorneys often attempt to create doubt by attacking the testimony of expert

An expert knowledge of forensic investigation procedures enhances the testimony of a forensic scientist.

witnesses, so being prepared and confident in public speaking is of great benefit. Most colleges offer public-speaking and seminar courses that expose students to the pressures of standing before an audience and giving a presentation, then answering questions related to the subject of their speech. The more practice a person has speaking in front of others, the better able she will be to thrive under the pressure of doing so.

In addition to public-speaking courses, forensic experts should have a basic understanding of legal proceedings. Introductory law classes are a good way to get exposure to the rules of law. The main focus of a forensic scientist should be on the rules of evidence, because improperly handled evidence, even if it is the most important piece of evidence available, is usually thrown out of court, damaging the case. The rules are very strict, and the slightest mishandling of evidence can effectively end a trial. It is obviously in the best interest of every forensic scientist to avoid this.

Some universities now offer forensic science as a major for students wishing to seek employment in this field. The coursework built into the cur-

Public-speaking skills help the credibility of expert testimony.

Working with Mark and Trace Evidence

riculum of these majors is varied and designed to introduce students to all of the topics that are critical for being a forensic scientist. Typically, these programs are four-year progressions that gradually increase in difficulty and complexity as the student becomes more familiar and comfortable with the information he needs to excel in the field. In addition to coursework, forensic science majors often include internships with local or regional crime laboratories, a vital part of a good forensic preparatory pathway.

Internships

Internships are perhaps the single best way to get an inside look at what is needed to succeed in any career, including forensic science. Coursework can be valuable, but it's often difficult to relate the work being done in a

Law classes are helpful in preparing for a career in forensic science.

The experience gained during an internship can help you decide whether a particular career is for you.

classroom to its use in real life. Students sometimes wonder why they must take a particular class; internships can help them understand why they need the wide variety of courses they must take. In addition, internships are valuable because it is very difficult to decide whether a particular career is the right one until being immersed in the career environment for a while.

Working with Mark and Trace Evidence

Without this experience, students may graduate and discover they are not happy in the field they have chosen.

Most forensic laboratories around the country have a number of internship positions open at various times of the year. Internships usually last for a specific number of weeks, so the laboratory can rotate interns all year long. Most internships are scheduled around college breaks, so students will not have to juggle working in the laboratory with their class schedule.

Internships are often scheduled around college breaks, so students will not have to juggle lab work and class work.

In some cases, the internship will be a paid position, but for the most part, interns are not paid for their work; the experience alone is considered adequate compensation. (Forensic laboratories accept interns as a way to foster growth in the profession, not because they get free work out of the interns; an inexperienced intern in the lab often means more work for those who are responsible for supervising and teaching her.) Internships are probably the best way to get a glimpse of the daily routines and tasks of a criminalist.

A criminalist may spend the majority of the day writing reports and reviewing caseloads.

Working with Mark and Trace Evidence   **93**

CASE STUDY: SMALL-TOWN MURDER

The small town of Humboldt, Nebraska, was rocked by a violent crime on December 31, 1994, when Anna Mae Lambert drove to the rented house used by her daughter just outside of town. She let herself in, as she always did, and discovered a horrible scene. She called the police.

When the sheriff's deputy arrived at the house, he found first a young man, then two young women dead in the bedroom; all had been shot to death. The deputy quickly ruled out suicide and called for Sheriff Laux, who identified two of the victims. Teena Brandon had been shot at close range (she had powder burns underneath her chin), while Lisa Lambert, the other woman, had been shot through the eye.

The sheriff called in the Nebraska State ECU to examine the crime scene. The ECU found a large amount of evidence at the scene, including several bullet casings, blood, shoe prints, and tire tracks. Police named several recently released sexual offenders as prime suspects in the case, but these men were quickly cleared.

As time passed, the story unfolded for the investigators. Teena Brandon often passed herself off as Brandon Teena. Posing as a man, she dated girls and appeared to have met someone she could trust in Lisa Lambert. At a party on Christmas Eve, when the truth about Brandon was revealed to a group of her friends, the revelation was followed by outrage. Two of the young men drank heavily and began harassing Brandon. One of them ended the night by raping her.

Brandon went to the hospital reluctantly. The nurses at the hospital gathered evidence with their rape kit, and sent the information on to Richardson County Sheriff Charles B. Laux. In his reports, Laux referred to Brandon as "it," and when he interviewed Brandon, she became upset by Laux's line of questions. She felt they were inappropriate and insulting, and she refused to answer many. Laux listed her as "uncooperative." She filed a complaint against him with his supervisors.

Three days later, sheriff's deputies started to go arrest the two men involved in the rape. Laux refused to allow them to go. This delay gave the men time to find Brandon and plot their revenge against her. The result was the death of three people: Teena, Lisa, and another friend who was staying with them.

A long list of evidence was collected against the two men, including the murder weapon. The tire impressions were linked to the car driven by one of the two. The shoe print was connected to Tom Nissen. The gun, which had been thrown in a river, had the name of John Lotter engraved on the handle. It was pretty clear that the men were going to jail. A confession sealed the case. The victims' families sued Laux for his "actions." A jury awarded the families monetary damages in connection with the actions of Sheriff Laux. Criminalists' work helped bring justice to unjust circumstances that had led to terrible tragedy.In 1903, the New York State prison system began the first systematic use of fingerprints for identification in the United States.

A Day in the
Life of a Criminalist

Despite the dramatic stories seen on television, the typical day for a criminalist may seem, at first glance, rather boring. He arrives at the crime laboratory, passes through security, goes to his station, and looks over the caseload for the day. He may have a backlog of trace evidence to examine and store. Writing various reports can also take up a good portion of each day. Criminalists rarely work alone in the forensic laboratory. In most cases, several criminalists work as a team on the varied pieces of evidence.

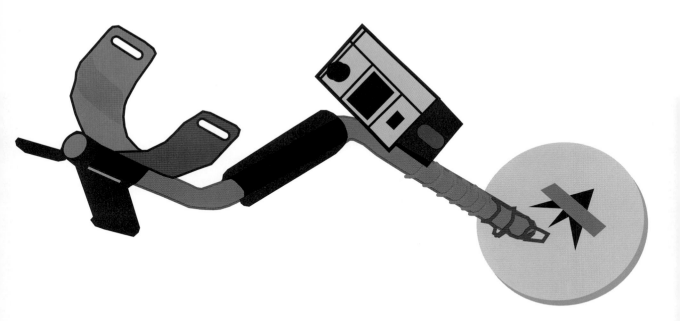

Metal detectors are often used to search for evidence.

Levels of Certification

Most crime laboratories have at least two different levels of criminalist on their staff. Because of the importance of the work they do, criminalists are usually classified by their level of experience. Criminalist I, the entry-level class, often includes new employees and those lacking experience. Criminalist IIs are the experts, well trained and prepared to handle nearly any evidence. Individuals classified as Criminalist I work under the supervision of those qualified as Criminalist II. In general, the tasks assigned to Criminalist I include the simpler, more routine examinations, and jobs such as preparing chemical solutions and maintaining equipment. Entry-level criminalists spend almost all their time working alongside a more experienced individual, gaining experience but not being left to work on critical evidence alone.

The qualifications for Criminalist I are easily met by a person having graduated from a four-year college with a science degree. It is very impor-

Criminalist I

- entry-level employee
- perform duties with help of other scientists
- conduct routine examinations, monitor proper functioning of equipment, make sure supplies are stocked

Criminalist II

- experts of forensic analysis
- may handle crucial evidence alone
- conduct elaborate investigations on crucial evidence, may testify as expert witness in court

In forensic science, few people have the qualifications and fame of Dr. Henry Lee. An immigrant to the United States from Taiwan, Dr. Lee worked hard to become the foremost authority in forensics in the country. He has worked on more than 6,000 cases in his career, including notable ones like the O.J. Simpson murder case, the Jon-Benet Ramsey murder, and the JFK assassination. His education and experience make him one of the most sought after forensic science experts in the world.

tant for every criminalist to have a strong understanding of the theories and methods of analysis of the major sciences. In addition, a Criminalist I must be comfortable working with statistics and other mathematical principles. A basic understanding of the operation of the major pieces of equipment commonly used in a crime laboratory is very important. The ability and knowledge to work safely with a wide variety of chemical compounds is vital as well.

The daily routines of a Criminalist I revolve around developing his skills and working to advance to Criminalist II. In order to advance to the next level of certification, a Criminalist I must prove he can perform all of the duties of the Criminalist II, in addition to being fully aware of the rules of the law and being prepared to be called as witness in court trials. Criminalist II certification requires that the individual be able to work alone, and to teach others the basics of the job. The work performed by a Criminalist II is often innovative and nonstandard. When there is evidence that requires special techniques, it is given to the Criminalist II. To attain this level of certification, a Criminalist I must prove she can perform all the tasks that might be required in the crime laboratory.

Major Tasks of the Criminalist

Each level of criminalist has a specific array of jobs that the professional with that certification needs to be comfortable performing on a regular basis. A critical aspect of the work is the maintenance of the laboratory equipment. If a piece of equipment is found to be out of calibration, a case can be thrown out of court. Criminalists often test the equipment with standard samples each day before they start their work with evidence. This procedure can effectively rule out calibration errors. In addition to this, the

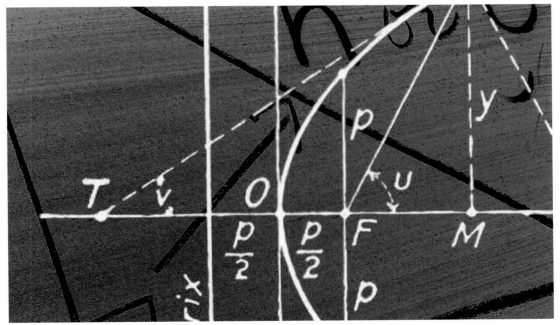

A Criminalist I must be comfortable working with mathematics.

Working with Mark and Trace Evidence

examinations usually are run with controls to show that the equipment is not the source of any errors.

Criminalists constantly handle evidence in the laboratory. They must protect the chain of custody, making sure to sign out the evidence each and every time they handle it. They check the accuracy of the information gathered from the crime scene, comparing the evidence to the photographs and sketches produced by the ECU. Everything must make sense in connection with the crime-scene analysis. As trace evidence is brought to the laboratory, it is the job of a criminalist to determine which tests are appropriate for the individual pieces of evidence.

Each bit of evidence is treated individually, tested in a variety of ways to gather as much information as possible. Criminalists perform analyses on a wide variety of materials brought into the laboratory, ranging from chemical to physical. The criminalist may be in charge of chemically separating different types of evidence. For example, in cases where arson is expected, investigators are particularly interested in the presence or absence of accelerants (highly flammable substances used to start the fire). A criminalist can often isolate traces of accelerant from a pile of ashes by subjecting the ashes to certain chemical tests. Burnt accelerant leaves a particular residue, and the criminalist knows how to find it.

Criminalists are required to prepare the *chemical reagents* for each task they need to perform. Some can be stored long term, while others need to be prepared fresh every single day. Entry-level criminalists usually prepare these solutions. In addition to preparing the chemicals, criminalists are often expected to maintain the laboratory stocks of the reagents. Ordering supplies for a laboratory can be surprisingly time consuming.

Outside the crime laboratory, the criminalist has a number of jobs as well. Criminalists are often sent to train police personnel so that police can better understand the work that is performed in the trace-evidence laboratory. When called to testify in court cases, a criminalist must be prepared to present the evidence clearly and quickly, and in a way that a jury with little knowledge of the subject can understand. She must appear professional and prepared, because the impression that can be made on the jury by a poorly dressed or unprepared criminalist can alter the outcome of a case.

Other Tasks of a Criminalist

Every criminalist is expected to spend time reviewing cases in which he is not directly involved to ensure he is prepared for the twists that a variety of crimes can present. A current knowledge of techniques and advances in the field of forensic science can be important in each case a criminalist works. Criminalists sometimes work independently in the laboratory on developing new techniques for examining evidence. If a criminalist discovers a new method of analysis, he is expected to publish the findings in a major forensic journal, such as the *Journal of Forensic Science*, so that others may

A typical crime laboratory uses thousands of dollars worth of chemical reagents every single day. It is an important task of a criminalist to check these chemicals and make sure they are not outdated. (Scientific supply companies can accidentally ship old chemicals to a laboratory.) Double-checking chemical stocks can save the laboratory thousands of dollars and prevent costly errors.

Important data may be found even after a piece of evidence has been burned or charred.

read and use his techniques. Other crime labs will review the newly developed techniques to make sure that no errors or faulty steps mar the process.

Criminalists are often called on by attorneys and judges to present seminars to educate others about the uses of trace-evidence analysis. State lawmakers must be kept updated on new developments and are interested in the work of employees in a crime laboratory. In addition, criminalists may

Special chemicals aid the task of analyzing samples of trace evidence.

Working with Mark and Trace Evidence   **103**

work closely with FBI officials to update the FBI handbook, a collection of standard methods used by many states in the processing of evidence. Keeping the handbook updated can be one of the most important tasks of a forensic scientist. When many criminalists use a method, it becomes more acceptable in court.

Criminalistics is perhaps the most variable of all the forensic disciplines. Few other forensic experts can claim to work with as many different types of evidence or with as many different techniques. The criminalist is somewhat of a jack-of-all-trades in the laboratory, able to tease more information out

A forensic scientist is truly a "jack-of-all-trades."

of tiny marks and traces than seems humanly possible. Criminalistic work has been instrumental in solving countless cases over the last century. As time passes and technology advances, the field will undoubtedly continue to grow in scope and importance.

Glossary

biased: Unable or unwilling to form a fair or objective opinion about somebody or something.

calibrating: Testing and adjusting the accuracy of a measuring instrument or process.

chain of custody: The documentation of who has the evidence at each step of an investigation.

chemical reagents: Substances used in a chemical reaction.

civil: Involving individuals or groups in legal action with each other or with the state, in which the penalty is usually a monetary award rather than incarceration.

common origin: Coming from the same place.

criminal: Punishable as a crime under the law, in which the penalty can include incarceration as well as fines.

genocide: The systematic killing of all the people from a national, ethnic, or religious group, or an attempt to do so.

impartial: Not favoring one person or one side over another.

impound: To take goods or possessions into official custody.

index of refraction: The speed of light in a vacuum divided by the speed of light through substances such as glass.

objective: Free of prejudice caused by personal feelings.

oblique: Slanting away from a surface plane.

redundancy: Duplication of information as a back up.

serologists: Scientists who study blood serum and its components.

standardized: Removed variations and irregularities and made all types or examples of something the same.

striations: Parallel grooves or narrow bands.

tool marks: The marks left by tools that can often be traced back to particular implements.

Further Reading

Camenson, Bythe. *Opportunities in Forensic Science Careers*. New York: McGraw-Hill, 2009.

Evans, Colin. *The Casebook of Forensic Detection: How Science Solved 100 of the World's Most Baffling Crimes*. New York: Berkley Trade, 2007.

Evans, Colin. A *Question of Evidence: The Casebook of Great Forensic Controversies, From Napoleon to O. J. Hoboken*, N.J.: Wiley, 2002.

Genge, Ngaire. *The Forensic Casebook: The Science of Crime Scene Investigation*. New York: Ballantine Books, 2002.

Houck, Max M. *Mute Witnesses: Trace Evidence Analysis*. San Diego, Calif.: Academic Press, 2001.

Houck, Max M. *Trace Evidence Analysis: More Cases in Forensic Microscopy and Mute Witnesses*. San Diego, Calif.: Academic Press, 2001.

Lyle, Douglas P. *Forensics for Dummies*. Hoboken, N.J.: For Dummies, 2004.

Miller, Hugh. *What the Corpse Revealed: Murder and the Science of Forensic Detection*. New York: St. Martin's True Crime Classics, 2000.

Morgan, Marilyn. *Careers in Criminology*. New York: McGraw-Hill, 2000.

Platt, Richard. *Crime Scene: The Ultimate Guide to Forensic Science*. New York: DK Publishing, 2003.

Ramsland, Katherine M. *The Forensic Science of C.S.I.* Berkeley, Calif.: Berkeley Publishing Group, 2001.

Saferstein, Richard. *Criminalistics: An Introduction to Forensic Science.* Englewood Cliffs, N.J.: Prentice Hall, 2010.

For More Information

Carpenter's Forensic Science Resources
www.tncrimlaw.com/forensic/f_criminalistics.html

FAQS–NEAFS
www.neafs.org/faqs.htm

Forensic Science, Forensics, and Investigation–Crimelibrary.com
www.crimelibrary.com/criminal_mind/forensics

From Fingerprints to DNA-ABC Science Online
www.abc.net.au/science/slab/forensic/default.htm

Introduction–FBI Forensic Handbook
www.fbi.gov/about-us/lab/handbook-of-forensic-services-pdf/view

Reddy's Forensic Home Page
www.forensicpage.com

Trace Evidence by Katherine Ramsland
www.crimelibrary.com/criminal_mind/forensics/trace/1.html

Publisher's note:
The websites listed on this page were active at the time of publication. The publisher is not responsible for websites that have changed their addresses or discontinued operation since the date of publication. The publisher will review and update the website list upon each reprint.

Index

Picture Credits

Benjamin Stewart: pp. 26, 58, 66, 75, 78, 79

Digital Vision: pp. 12, 18, 34

Evangeline Ehl: pp. 60, 62, 63, 69, 70, 104

MK Bassett-Harvey: p. 96

PhotoDisc: pp. 29, 88, 91, 93

Photos.com: pp. 10, 11, 15, 17, 23, 28, 30, 36, 38, 40, 42, 43, 52, 53, 64, 65, 67, 80, 84, 85, 89, 90, 92, 99, 102, 103

To the best knowledge of the publisher, all other images are in the public domain. If any image has been inadvertently uncredited, please notify Vestal Creative Services, Vestal, New York 13850, so that rectification can be made for future printings.

Biographies

AUTHOR

William is a high school biology and chemistry teacher in upstate New York. He is a graduate of the State University of New York at Buffalo, earning a master's degree in biology. His interest in forensic science led him to complete elective coursework in the forensic science training program at the University of New York at Buffalo. He has also been involved in the development and testing of a series of forensic science educational activities, as well as a comprehensive activity for a national science conference.

SERIES CONSULTANTS

Carla Miller Noziglia is Senior Forensic Advisor for the U.S. Department of Justice, International Criminal Investigative Training Assistant Program. A Fellow of the American Academy of Forensic Sciences, Ms. Noziglia served as chair of the board of Trustees of the Forensic Science Foundation. Her work has earned her many honors and commendations, including Distinguished Fellow from the American Academy of Forensic Sciences (2003) and the Paul L. Kirk Award from the American Academy of Forensic Sciences Criminalistics Section. Ms. Noziglia's publications include *The Real Crime Lab* (coeditor, 2005), *So You Want to be a Forensic Scientist* (coeditor, 2003), and contributions to *Drug Facilitated Sexual Assault* (2001), *Convicted by Juries, Exonerated by Science: Case Studies in the Use of DNA* (1996), and the *Journal of Police Science* (1989). She is on the editorial board of the *Journal for Forensic Identification*.

Jay Siegel is Director of the Forensic and Investigative Sciences Program at Indiana University-Purdue University, Indianapolis and Chair of the Department of Chemistry and Chemical Biology. He holds a Ph.D. in Analytical Chemistry from George Washington University. He worked for three years at the Virginia Bureau of Forensic Sciences, analyzing drugs, fire residues, and trace evidence. From 1980 to 2004 he was professor of forensic chemistry and director of the forensic science program at Michigan State University in the School of Criminal Justice. Dr. Siegel has testified over 200 times as an expert witness in twelve states, Federal Court and Military Court. He is editor in chief of the *Encyclopedia of Forensic Sciences*, author of *Forensic Science: A Beginner's Guide and Fundamentals of Forensic Science*, and he has more than thirty publications in forensic science journals. Dr. Siegel was awarded the 2005 Paul Kirk Award for lifetime achievement in forensic science. In February 2009, he was named Distinguished Fellow by the American Academy of Forensic Sciences.